SEARCHING ISSUES
ISSUES
COURSE MANUAL

Alpha

Alpha Resources
Alpha North America

TABLE OF CONTENTS

1
Why Does God Allow Suffering?

Introduction

Most frequently raised objection

Greatest single challenge to the Christian faith in every generation

- Global suffering
- Community suffering
- Individual suffering

Seeming contradiction between suffering and an all-loving, all-powerful God

I. Human freedom

Suffering not part of creation (Genesis 1-2, Revelation 21)

Sin of Adam and Eve led to beginning of suffering.

All suffering is a result of sin, directly or indirectly.

Reasons for and consequences of free will:

1) Our own sin

   Suffering can be:

   - inevitable consequence

Notes

e.g., drug abuse, reckless driving

- God actively judging (2 Kings 5:27; Acts 5:1-11)

  No automatic link between sin and suffering (Job 42:7-8)

  Jesus expressly repudiates automatic link. (Luke 13:1-5; John 9:1-3)

  Extra distinction: (1 Peter 2:19-20)

  Danger of making judgements about others' suffering

2) Sin of others

- Global: e.g., war, starvation
- Community: e.g., Dunblane (1996), Aberfan (1966)
- Individual: e.g., murder, adultery, theft, abuse, unloving parents

3) Sin of Adam

- Disorder in creation—fallen world (Genesis 3:18; Romans 8:20)
- Natural disasters

Freedom explains the origin of suffering but does not answer the question, "Why me?"

II. GOD WORKS THROUGH SUFFERING

He uses it for good:

- Draws us to Christ
- Brings us to Christian maturity (Hebrews 5:8)

  -Disciplining toward holiness (Hebrews 12:10, 11)

  -Refining toward purity (1 Peter 1:7)

  -Pruning toward fruitfulness (John 15:2)

- Brings about His purposes (Romans 8:28; Genesis 50:20)
- Some suffering we cannot comprehend.

III. GOD MORE THAN COMPENSATES FOR OUR SUFFERING

For some in this life: e.g., Joseph, Job

For all Christians, there is the hope of heaven. (Romans 8:18; 2 Corinthians 4:17)

Maintaining an eternal perspective —a new heaven and a new earth (Revelation 21:1)

Notes

CONCLUSION

How do we respond?

- Three questions to ask God:

  -Is this suffering a result of my own sin? (If so, ask for God's forgiveness and cleansing.)

  -What are You saying to me through this?

  -What do You want me to do?

- Hold on to our hope (Hebrews 12:2).

- When we see others suffering, we are called to show compassion and take action.

- Resist suffering as alien intrusion in God's world.

- Come back to the cross (God suffering for us and with us) of Christ and His resurrection (the promise of eternity).

2
WHAT ABOUT OTHER RELIGIONS?

INTRODUCTION

Statistics: Encyclopedia Britannica

- 1900 million Christians = 32.9% of world population
- 880 million Muslims
- 663 million Hindus
- 311 million Buddhists

Many other smaller groupings

Atheists = 4.5% of world population

I. IS JESUS THE ONLY WAY TO GOD?

The New Testament answer: "yes"

(John 14:6)

(1 Timothy 2:5)

(Acts 4:12)

(Hebrews 2:3)

Notes

What makes Jesus unique?

- His qualification (Acts 3:14)
- His achievement (Acts 4:12)
- His resurrection (Acts 4:10)

II. WHAT DO WE SAY ABOUT OTHER RELIGIONS?

Jesus: "I am the truth"

Jesus is the standard by which all truth claims are to be tested. But we would expect to find truth in other religions for at least three reasons:

- God has partially revealed Himself in creation (Psalm 19:1, Romans 1:20).
- Human beings are made in the image of God. We have been given a conscience with which to distinguish right and wrong (Romans 2:14-15).
- In every human heart there is a hunger for God (Ecclesiastes 3:11).

III. What about those who have never heard about Jesus?

- Hypothetical question—can only be asked by someone who *has* heard about Jesus.

- We can be sure God will be just (Genesis 18:25).

- No one will be saved by his or her religion (Ephesians 2:8).

- It is possible to be saved by grace through faith even if someone has never heard of Jesus (Romans 4:3; Romans 4:6, Luke 18:9-14).

- There are biblical grounds for great optimism (Genesis 22:17; Romans 5:2).

IV. Why should we bother to tell others about Jesus?

- The glory of Jesus Christ is at stake.

- Jesus commanded us to go into all the world and tell the good news.

- Without knowing about Jesus no one can have assurance of forgiveness and the abundant life He offers.

Notes

Notes

CONCLUSION

Our response must be to tell people the good news about Jesus.

- Be humble
- Be sensitive
- Be positive
- Be respectful
- Be courageous

3

IS THERE ANYTHING WRONG WITH SEX BEFORE MARRIAGE?

INTRODUCTION

Obsession of the modern era

Concurrent breakdown in family life

Repressive attitude of former times

What is the biblical understanding?

I. GOD, IN HIS LOVE, HAS GIVEN US A GOOD PLAN

- The Bible affirms our sexuality (Genesis 1:27).

  -The body is good (Psalm 139:14).

  -The sexual urge is God-given (Genesis 2:25).

- The Bible celebrates sexual intimacy (Genesis 4:1).

  -*Song of Songs*: delight, tenderness, contentment and satisfaction

- Sex in its right context is good and beautiful (Ephesians 5).

- The biblical context for sexual intercourse is the life-long commitment in marriage between one man and one woman.

  Creation account (Genesis 2:24)

  (Matthew 19:5-6)

  -Leaving

  -Uniting

  -"One flesh" sexual union

- Partnership and procreation are linked (Genesis 1:28).

II. GOD, IN HIS LOVE, WARNS AGAINST HUMAN DISTORTIONS

- Sin affects every area of human lives, including sexuality (Romans 3:23).

  None of us is in a position to pass judgement (John 8:7).

  Nevertheless sin does matter (John 8:11).

- Any sex outside marriage is a distortion of God's good gift and falls short of His ideal.

  This includes adultery and sex before marriage (1 Corinthians 6:16, 18; Mark 7:21; 1 Thessalonians 4:3-8).

- When God's pattern is broken, people get hurt.

  -We risk hurting ourselves.

  -We risk hurting others.

  -We risk hurting society.

  -We hurt God.

God will judge all sin (1 Thessalonians 4:6).

III. GOD, IN HIS LOVE, SENT JESUS TO RESTORE US

Jesus did not come to condemn the world but to save it, giving us the power to resist temptation, and bring forgiveness and healing. (God can enable individuals to control their sexual urges.)

How to resist:

- Jesus began with the heart, the eyes and the thoughts (Matthew 5:28).

Notes

- We need to help one another by not putting temptation in the way.

- Is masturbation a way out?

  Not physically harmful and it is nowhere specifically condemned in the Bible.

  Three concerns:

  -Tendency to become obsessive

  -Depersonalizes sex

  -Often associated with lustful thoughts

Forgiveness

- All of us have failed in this area to greater or lesser extent.

- Way to receive forgiveness is through repentance (Psalm 51).

CONCLUSION

The heart of our sexuality is not the biological dimension but the personal one.

Christians must worship God Himself, not His gifts.

- If we treat pleasure as a god, in the long-run we find emptiness, disappointment, and addiction.

- If we seek God, we find complete fulfillment.

4
HOW DOES THE NEW AGE MOVEMENT RELATE TO CHRISTIANITY?

INTRODUCTION

Cultural shift from "Enlighten-ment" to "Post-modernity"

One strand is New Age movement.

Emphasizes experience and values spirituality.

Highlights emptiness and shortcomings of rationalism and materialism.

I. WHAT IS THE NEW AGE MOVEMENT?

Umbrella term that covers various diverse movements, beliefs and lifestyles. Impossible to define—no leader, no organization, no headquarters.

Mixture of Eastern mysticism and occult practices which have been given a Western materialistic flavor.

May include self-improvement programs, holistic health, concern for world peace, ecology and spiritual enlightenment

NOTE:

- Many New Age teachings are derived from Eastern mysticism, TM, reincarnation, karma, Zen, yoga and levitation.

- Influence of nature religions from around the world, including Druidism and Wicca witchcraft

- A number of practices in the movement overtly occult and condemned in the Bible: e.g., astrology (horoscopes), fortune-telling, clairvoyance, consulting the dead, spiritism, mediums, channelling, spirit guides and tarot cards

  -(Deuteronomy 18:10)

  -(Leviticus 19:26, 31)

  -(Galatians 5:20)

  -(Revelation 9:20-21)

  Influence of the movement everywhere: arts and music, bookshops, international capitalism, films, videos and computer games, even church

II. What are the beliefs of the New Age movement?

John Stott's summary

- All is God—"pantheism"

  -No distinction between the Creator and what He has created

  -A self-centered movement: God within us

  -Focus on self—opposite of Christianity

- All is one—"monism"

  -Rejection of moral absolutes

  -"Sin" is not a popular word

  -Guidance comes from "within"—"if it feels good, do it."

  -Everyone is eventually making progress onward and upward toward spiritual enlightenment and perfection. No judgement— contrary to Christianity (Genesis 3:4; Hebrews 9:27)

- All is well—optimism

  Evolutionary progress toward Utopia

Notes

_____
_____
_____
_____
_____
_____
_____
_____
_____
_____
_____
_____
_____
_____
_____
_____
_____
_____
_____
_____
_____
_____

Notes

III. WHAT IS WRONG WITH THE NEW AGE MOVEMENT?

Some things linked to the New Age movement are themselves good, such as:

- The challenge to prevailing materialism and rationalism
- The emphasis on the importance of experience and the high value put on spirituality
- The focus on compassion, love and unity
- The search for spiritual reality

But it falls way short of the glorious truths of Christianity:

1) It does not get near the truth about God the Father.

- God is thought of as an impersonal, abstract force.
- Men and women were made to live in a personal relationship of love and worship of God

"You have made us yourself, and our heart is restless until it rests in you."

St. Augustine

2) It does not get near the truth about God the Son.

- Jesus is seen merely as one of the "ascended masters", along with Buddha, Krishna and others.

- Jesus Christ is in fact *"the way, and the truth and the life"* (John 14:6).

- New Age discounts the cross and resurrection—the only true means of salvation.

3) It does not get near the truth about God the Holy Spirit.

- The search for spiritual power, spiritual experience and transformed lives is fruitless without the Holy Spirit.

- The Holy Spirit transforms Christians into the likeness of Jesus Christ and enables them to have an impact on society (2 Corinthians 3:18 Galatians 5:22-23).

Notes

_____

_____

_____

_____

_____

_____

_____

_____

_____

_____

_____

_____

_____

_____

_____

_____

_____

_____

_____

Notes	## Conclusion
	What response should we make?

Conclusion

What response should we make?

1) Need for a double repentance:

- If we've been involved in New Age practices we need to ask God's forgiveness, turn to Jesus Christ and ask the Holy Spirit to come and live in our lives.

- Those of us involved in the church need to repent of our rigidity, rationalism and failure to make the church relevant to the culture in which we live.

2) We need to soak ourselves in the truth (Colossians 2:8; 2 Timothy 4:3-5).

C. We need to bring the good news of Jesus to those who are involved in the New Age, demonstrating by our lives (both individually and as the church) the supernatural power of God: Father, Son, and Holy Spirit.

5
WHAT IS THE CHRISTIAN ATTITUDE TOWARD HOMOSEXUALITY?

INTRODUCTION

The Bible is the story of God's love for all humanity. God loves all people, irrespective of race, color, background or sexual orientation. As we approach this subject, we must be conscious of the agony that exists for many people in this area. Jesus came not to condemn us, but to save (John 3:17). In the same way, the Christian community needs to carefully show sensitivity and understanding toward those for whom their homosexual orientation is a daily struggle, and to affirm them as human beings loved by God.

The gay liberation movement "urges the view that homosexuality is a natural variant of human sexuality—as natural as red hair or left-handedness—to be affirmed and rejoiced in, and that its expression in fully loving physical sexual embrace is well within the purpose and will of God."

Notes

Notes

I. Is homosexual practice an option for a Christian?

Biblical view of sexual intercourse is positive and liberating.

Context is lifelong commitment (in marriage) between one man and one woman (Genesis 2: 24).

Our bodies were not designed for homosexual intercourse.

The view of marriage and sex, which Jesus quoted and endorsed, rules out all sex outside marriage, whether heterosexual or homosexual.

All references to homosexual practice in the Bible are negative:

- (Leviticus 18:22; 20:13)
- (Judges 19:23)
- (1 Corinthians 6:9-10; 1 Timothy 1:9)
- (1 Corinthians 6:11)
- (Romans 1:24-27)

Nowhere does the Bible condemn homosexual orientation, homosexual feelings or homosexual temptation.

Temptation is not sin (Hebrews 4:15).

The Bible does not condemn homosexual preference, but homosexual practice.

II. IS AIDS THE JUDGEMENT OF GOD ON HOMOSEXUAL PRACTICE?

We can look at biblical principles and seek to apply them to a modern disease.

Two different types of judgement:

1) *"effectus"*—inevitable result of sin

2) *"affectus"*—God's personal reaction against sin.

Is AIDS "effectus" or "affectus"?

- One day God will judge the world—He will be perfectly fair and just.

- God sometimes intervenes as a judge in this life (Genesis 19; Acts 5).

Notes

- Supernatural acts of intervening judgement are rare, but His judgement in the sense of the inevitable results of sin is ongoing.

AIDS cannot be seen as a one-off judgement of God "affectus" on homosexuality since 90-percent of the new infections world-wide are heterosexual.

Some are infected through blood transfusions and others inherit from their parents.

However, AIDS can be seen as a consequence of breaking God's rules relating to sexual morality— "effectus."

God's rules were given to protect people from getting hurt.

When His laws are broken, it is often not only the law breaker who is hurt, but innocent people too.

We were not designed for homosexual or promiscuous activity.

Best way to stop spread of AIDS: return to biblical standards

AIDS only a symptom of real crisis in society—separation from God

III. WHAT IS THE WAY FORWARD?

- The New Testament promises total forgiveness through the cross of Christ.

- There is no condemnation for the man or woman who repents and seeks to obey Christ (Romans 8:1).

- Homosexual practice is not the worst sin, nor is it unforgivable (1 Corinthians 6:11).

- Paul suggested his readers have changed and given up their former practices.

- God's promise = "no temptation has seized you except what is common among people." But when you are tempted, He will also provide a way out so that you can stand up under it (1 Corinthians 10:13).

- Those who fight their desire for homosexual behavior through the power of the Holy Spirit are "more than conquerors through Christ who strengthens them" (Romans 8:37).

Christopher Townsend:
"Our true humanity does not ultimately rest in our sexuality but in fulfilling our capacity for personal communion with God."

Notes

IV. WHAT SHOULD OUR ATTITUDE BE TO THOSE INVOLVED IN A HOMOSEXUAL LIFESTYLE?

We are all fallen: none of us is in a position to throw stones at others (John 8:7).

Our calling is to follow Christ's example, which is to love and accept people unconditionally.

At the same time, we must recognize sin as sin, rather than condoning it (John 8:11); this is part of love.

- Speak out where appropriate against the PRACTICE of homosexuality.

- Love *all* people and welcome them with open arms into the church.

- Promote a safe environment where the homosexually oriented can find somebody with whom they can talk and pray.

- The church should be at the forefront of bringing hope and healing to those with AIDS.

CONCLUSION

Love is the key from first to last.

- In His love, God gave us sex.

- In His love, He also gave us boundaries.

- In His love, He sent Jesus to bring us forgiveness and the power to resist temptation and bring us healing.

We are called to be like Him and to go out and love as He loved us.

Notes

6
IS THERE A CONFLICT BETWEEN SCIENCE AND CHRISTIANITY?

INTRODUCTION

Popular belief is that science and Christianity are in direct conflict.

Two reasons:

1) Times in history when the church has opposed the results of scientific study: e.g., Galileo and the Roman Catholic Church

2) Popular thinking that modern scientific study explains everything that was once explained by belief in God

I. SCIENCE AND CHRISTIAN FAITH ARE NOT INCOMPATIBLE

The Christian worldview provided the right environment for modern science to emerge.

- The Christian faith is monotheistic.

  Belief in one God led people to expect a uniformity in nature, with the underlying laws of nature remaining the same in space and time.

- The Christian doctrine of creation by a rational God of order led scientists to expect a world which was both ordered and intelligible.

- The Christian belief in a transcendent God, separate from nature, meant that experimentation was justified.

For much of history Christianity and scientific study have been allies not opponents.

- Copernicus (1473-1543)

- Galileo (1564-1642)

- Kepler (1571-1630)

- Newton (1642-1727)

- Faraday (1791-1867)

- Robert Boyle, Joseph Lister, Louis Pasteur, Gregor Mendel, Lord Kelvin, James Maxwell, James Simpson

Notes

II. Science and Scripture do not contradict each other

Alleged conflicts between science and theology:

- Spinoza (1632-1677): nothing can "contravene nature's universal laws"

- Hume: a miracle is "a violation of the laws of nature" and consequently impossible (circular argument: supernatural ruled out from start)

1) Miracles

A knowledge of laws of nature essential in order to recognize miracles: i.e., not natural for someone to rise from the dead.

The real issue is: "Is there a God?" If there is, then miracles become a real possibility.

"I'm not suggesting that miracles are an adequate basis for theism. But, once we have come on other grounds to believe in God... it becomes logical to affirm, and illogical to deny, the possibility of the miraculous. For 'natural laws' describe God's activity; they do not control it."

John Stott

2) Evolution

Much of the theory of evolution is still only a theory.

- Micro-evolution: development within a species—could not conceivably be said to conflict with the Bible.

- Macro-evolution: evolution from one species to another (e.g., apes to humans). Still unproven and remains a theory which is not accepted by all scientists.

There are many different interpretations of Genesis held by sincere Christians.

- Literal six-day creation

- Others point out that the Hebrew word "day"has many different meanings, even within Scripture—can mean a long period of time

- Others see Genesis 1 not necessarily connected with chronological events in history. It is a pre-scientific and non-scientific account of creation, dealing with matters outside the scope of science.

Notes

Main point of Genesis 1 is not to answer the questions "How?" and "When?" (scientific), but the questions "Why?" and "Who?" (theological questions).

The Bible offers a personal explanation rather than a scientific one.

III. SCIENCE AND SCRIPTURE COMPLEMENT EACH OTHER

Science is the study of God's general self-revelation in creation.

Biblical theology is the study of God's "special" revelation in Jesus.

(Psalm 19:1-4a; Romans 1:20; Acts 14:17; 17:22-28)

"Science without religion is lame."

Einstein

God has made a world where there is much to suggest His presence:

- Causation argument
- Evidence of design

General revelation suggests the tremendous power, intelligence and imagination of a personal creator.

- We cannot find the God of the Bible through science alone. Only by God's special revelation can we find *"the God and Father of our Lord Jesus Christ."*

- Science cannot speak to the deepest needs of men and women (including scientists).

  -It cannot deal with the problems of loneliness or hearts broken by grief.

  -No answer to moral dilemmas

  -No remedy for the problem of unforgiven sin and guilt

Only in the cross of Christ do we find the answer to these problems.

CONCLUSION

We need science and scientists. Our civilization owes a great deal to their work. But, more importantly, we need Christianity and Jesus Christ.

Notes

7
IS THE TRINITY UNBIBLICAL, UNBELIEVABLE AND IRRELEVANT?

INTRODUCTION

Derived from the Latin word "trinitas," which means "threeness"

Tri-personality of God

I. IS IT BIBLICAL?

The word "Trinity" does not appear in the Bible.

First used in its Greek form by Theophilus, Bishop of Antioch in AD 180.

"Let us not be misled by the foolish argument that because the term 'Trinity' does not occur in the scriptures, the doctrine of the Trinity is therefore unscriptural."

F.F. Bruce

Christianity arose out of Judaism—monotheistic faith. New Testament affirms only one God.

(John 5:44; Romans 3:30; 1 Timothy 1:17; James 2:19)

Early Christians faced two historical events which revolutionized their understanding of God:

- The revelatory events of the life, death, and resurrection of Jesus Christ

- The experience of the Holy Spirit at Pentecost

Came to believe in the deity of the Father, the deity of the Son and the deity of the Holy Spirit: yet they still believed there was only one God. (See John's gospel.)

Concept of Trinity permeates pages of New Testament.

Some suggest hint in Old Testament (Genesis 1:1-3a).

New Testament: several trinitarian formulae:

- Baptism into the name (singular) of the Father and the Son and the Holy Spirit (Matthew 28:19)

- The Grace (2 Corinthians 13:14)

Notes

While these two texts do not expressly state the doctrine of the Trinity, they point strongly toward it.

- Paul sees virtually every aspect of the Christian faith and Christian life in trinitarian terms:

  -Gifts of the Spirit (1 Corinthians 12:4-6)

  -Prayer (Ephesians 2:18)

  -Fullness of the Spirit (Ephesians 3:14-19)

  -Unity (Ephesians 4: 3-6)

  -Ethical instruction (Ephesians 4)

  -Worship (Ephesians 5:18-20)

  -Salvation (2 Thessalonians 2:13-14)

- Also Peter:

  -Election (1 Peter 1:1-2)

Yet, no formal credal statement about the Trinity

Early church forced into defining a coherent and systematic doctrine against the heretical views which were being expounded:

1) Polytheism

2) One person with three names (Sabellius reduced the Trinity to a unity with three modes of expression)

- Council of Constantinople in AD 381, building on the Council of Nicaea in AD 325, spoke of one God and three persons.

- Athanasian creed:

  "We worship one God in Trinity, and Trinity in Unity, neither confounding the Persons nor dividing the Divine Being. For there is one Person of the Father, another of the Son, and another the Holy Spirit: but the Godhead of the Father, the Son and the Holy Spirit is all one."

II. Is it believable?

Not easy to understand

Dealing with the nature of God Himself

Human analogies

- The triangle/shamrock/H2O
- The nature of the universe: space, time, and matter
- A book: in mind of author, on shelf in library, and in imagination of reader
- A house: architect, purchaser, and tenant

All analogies ultimately fall to the ground.

Three limits:

- Human language is limited.
- Limits of our own understanding and intellects
- Limits of our own finite world and our finite minds

III. Is it relevant?

Sheds light on the nature of God and His interaction with His creation

- The Trinity shows that God is self-sufficient and did not need to create in order to love and communicate.
- No single picture or image of God is good enough.

- It is the triune God who meets our most fundamental psychological needs as human beings.

- It teaches us that there is an inherent threefoldness about every act of God's revelation.

CONCLUSION

We can have a full experience of God:

- Experience of the Fatherhood of God (Romans 8:14-16)

- Experience of the love of Christ (Ephesians 3:14-19)

- Experience of the power of the Spirit (Ephesians 3:16; Acts 1:8)

Notes

Alpha Resources

Alpha—Questions of Life by Nicky Gumbel

What is the point of life?
What happens when we die?
Is forgiveness possible?
Who is Jesus?
What relevance does He have for our lives today?

In fifteen compelling chapters Nicky Gumbel tackles the answers
to these and other key questions, pointing the way to an authentic
Christianity that is exciting and relevant to today's world.

"Alpha—Questions of Life is a sympathetic, fascinating, and
immensely readable introduction to Jesus Christ—still the most
attractive and captivating person that it is possible to know. Nicky
Gumbel's informed approach ensures that the search for truth
fully engages our minds as well as our hearts."
(From the foreword by Sandy Miller.)
15396 ISBN: 0-7814-5261-9

Searching Issues by Nicky Gumbel

This book provides answers to the seven questions most often
asked during Alpha, including chapters on suffering, sex before
marriage, other religions, the New Age, and more.
15412 ISBN: 0-7814-5259-7

Why Jesus? by Nicky Gumbel

Many people today are puzzled about Jesus.

Why is there so much interest in a person born over 2,000 years ago?
Why are so many people excited about Jesus?
Why do we need Him? Why did He come? Why did He die?
Why should anyone bother to find out?

Nicky Gumbel tackles these issues in *Why Jesus?* a challenging, short presentation of Jesus Christ.

Nicky Gumbel studied law at Cambridge and theology at Oxford, practiced as a lawyer, and is now ordained and on the staff of Holy Trinity Brompton Church in London.
20073 ISBN: 1-931808-090

Why Christmas? by Nicky Gumbel

The Christmas edition of *Why Jesus?* This booklet makes an ideal Christmas gift and may be useful at a Christmas Alpha supper or guest service.
65755 ISBN: 1-931808-104

The God Who Changes Lives
Books 1-4

Edited by Mark Elsdon-Dew

Does God act in people's lives today?

Four volumes of stories from people whose lives have been dramatically touched by an encounter with God. Some tell of restored relationships; others how they have been given strength in the midst of pain.

These are books for anyone interested in whether God is there— and what He can do.

Volume 1, 16477 ISBN: 1-931808-120
Volume 2, 53314 ISBN: 1-931808-139
Volume 3, 100650 ISBN: 1-931808-147
Volume 4, The American Collection, 100651 ISBN: 1-931808-791

The God Who Changes Lives Video

As a young man, Paul Cowley ended up in prison and later, after a brief marriage, became estranged from his son Clinton. In this video Paul tells the remarkable story of how God changed his life and brought about reconciliation with his son.
97345 ISBN: 1-931808-341

More Alpha resources by Nicky Gumbel

Challenging Lifestyle
Studies in the Sermon on the Mount showing how Jesus' teaching flies in the face of modern lifestyle and presents us with a radical alternative.
25320 ISBN: 1-931808-163

A Life Worth Living
What happens after Alpha? Based on the book of Philippians, this is an invaluable next step for those who have just completed the Alpha course and for anyone eager to put his or her faith on a firm biblical footing.
15438 ISBN: 0-8547-6740-1

How to Run the Alpha Course: Telling Others
The theological principles and the practical details of how courses are run. Each alternate chapter consists of a testimony of someone whose life has been changed by God through the Alpha course.
16618 ISBN: 1-931808-21X

30 Days
Nicky Gumbel selects thirty passages from the Old and New Testament which can be read over thirty days. It is designed for those on the Alpha course and others who are interested in beginning to explore the Bible.
54056 ISBN: 1-931808-112

The Heart of Revival
Ten Bible studies based on the books of Isaiah, drawing out important truths for today by interpreting some of the teaching of the Old Testament prophet Isaiah. The book seeks to understand what revival might mean and how we can prepare to be part of it.
52894 ISBN: 1-931808-155

This book is an Alpha resource. The Alpha course is a practical introduction to the Christian faith initiated by Holy Trinity Brompton Church in London, and now being run by thousands of churches throughout the UK and around the world.

For more information on the Alpha course or Alpha resources, including books, tapes, videos, DVDs and training manuals, contact:

Alpha U.S.A.
74 Trinity Place
New York, NY 10006
Tel: 800 DO ALPHA
Tel: 800.362.5742
Fax: 212.406.7521
e-mail: info@alphausa.org
www.alphausa.org

Alpha Canada
1620 W. 8th Ave., Suite 300
Vancouver, BC V6J 1V4
Tel: 800.743.0899
Fax: 604.224.6124
e-mail: office@alphacanada.org
www.alphacanada.org

To purchase resources in Canada:

Cook Communications Ministries
P.O. Box 98, 55 Woodslee Avenue
Paris, ONT N3L 3E5
Tel: 800.263.2664
Fax: 800.461.8575
e-mail: custserv@cook.ca
www.cook.ca